GENE STRAT"

A LITTLE STORY OF HER LIFE AND WORK

GENE STRATTON-PORTER

A LITTLE STORY OF HER LIFE AND WORK

WILDSIDE PRESS

AT THE FOOT OF THE RAINBOW

GENE STRATTON-PORTER: A LITTLE STORY OF HER LIFE AND WORK

For several years Doubleday, Page & Company have been receiving repeated requests for information about the life and books of Gene Stratton-Porter. Her fascinating nature work with bird, flower, and moth, and the natural wonders of the Limberlost Swamp, made famous as the scene of her nature romances, all have stirred much curiosity among readers everywhere.

Mrs. Porter did not possess what has been called "an aptitude for personal publicity." Indeed, up to the present, she has discouraged quite successfully any attempt to stress the personal note. It is practically impossible, however, to do the kind of work she has done — to make genuine contributions to natural science by her wonderful field work among birds, insects, and flowers, and then, through her romances, to bring several hundred thousands of people to love and understand nature in a way they never did before — without arousing a legitimate interest in her own history, her ideals, her methods of work, and all that underlies the structure of her unusual achievement.

Her publishers have felt the pressure of this growing interest and it was at their request that she furnished the data for a biographical sketch that was to be written of her. But when this actually came to hand, the present compiler found that the author had told a story so much more interesting than anything he could write of her, that it became merely a question of how little need be added.

The following pages are therefore adapted from what might be styled the personal record of Gene Stratton-Porter. This will account for the very intimate picture of family life in the Middle West for some years following the Civil War.

Mark Stratton, the father of Gene Stratton-Porter, described his wife, at the time of their marriage, as a "ninety-pound bit of pink porcelain, pink as a wild rose, plump as a partridge, having a big rope of bright brown hair, never ill a day in her life, and bearing the loveliest name ever given a woman — Mary." He further added that "God fashioned her heart to be gracious, her body to be the mother of children, and as her especial gift of Grace, he put Flower Magic into her fingers." Mary Stratton was the mother of twelve lusty babies, all of whom she reared past eight years of age, losing two a little over that, through an attack of scarlet fever with whooping cough; too ugly a combination for even such a wonderful mother as she. With this brood on her hands she found time to keep an immaculate house, to set a table renowned in her part of the state, to entertain with unfailing hospitality all who came to her door, to beautify her home with such means as she could command, to embroider and fashion clothing by hand for her children; but her great gift was conceded by all to be the making of things to grow. At that she was wonderful. She started dainty little vines and climbing plants from tiny seeds she found in rice and coffee. Rooted things she soaked in water, rolled in fine sand, planted according to habit, and they almost never failed to justify her expectations. She even grew trees and shrubs from slips and cuttings no one else would have thought of trying to cultivate, her last resort being to cut a slip diagonally, insert the lower end in a small potato, and plant as if rooted. And it nearly always grew!

There is a shaft of white stone standing at her head in a cemetery that belonged to her on a corner of her husband's land; but to Mrs. Porter's mind her mother's real monument is a cedar of Lebanon which she set in the manner described above. The cedar tops the brow of a little hill crossing the grounds. She carried two slips from Ohio, where they were given to her by a man who had brought the trees as tiny things from the holy Land. She planted both in this way, one in her dooryard and one in her cemetery. The tree on the hill stands thirty feet tall now, topping all others, and has a trunk two feet in circumference.

Mrs. Porter's mother was of Dutch extraction, and like all Dutch women she worked her special magic with bulbs, which she favoured above other flowers. Tulips, daffodils, star flowers, lilies, dahlias, little bright hyacinths, that she called "blue bells," she dearly loved. From these she distilled exquisite perfume by putting clusters, & time of perfect bloom, in bowls lined with freshly made, unsalted butter, covering them closely, and cutting the few drops of extract thus obtained with alcohol. "She could do more different things," says the author, "and finish them all in a greater degree of perfection than any other woman I have ever known. If I were limited to one adjective in describing her, 'capable' would be the word."

The author's father was descended from a long line of ancestors of British blood. He was named for, and traced his origin to, that first Mark Stratton who lived in New York, married the famous beauty, Anne Hutchinson, and settled on Stratton Island, afterward corrupted to Staten, according to family tradition. From that point back for generations across the sea he followed his line to the family of Strattons of which the Earl of Northbrooke is the present head. To his British traditions and the customs of his family, Mark Stratton clung with rigid tenacity, never swerving from his course a particle under the influence of environment or association. All his ideas were clear-cut; no man could influence him against his better judgment. He believed in God, in courtesy, in honour, and cleanliness, in beauty, and in education. He used to say that he would rather see a child of his the author of a book of which he could be proud, than on the throne of England, which was the strongest way he knew to express himself. His very first earnings he spent for a book; when other men rested, he read; all his life he was a student of extraordinarily tenacious memory. He especially loved history: Rollands, Wilson's Outlines, Hume, Macauley, Gibbon, Prescott, and Bancroft, he could quote from all of them paragraphs at a time contrasting the views of different writers on a given event, and remembering dates with unfailing accuracy. "He could repeat the entire Bible," says Mrs. Stratton-Porter, "giving chapters and verses, save the books of Generations; these he said 'were a waste of gray matter to learn.' I never knew him to fail in telling where any verse quoted to him was to be found in the Bible." And she adds: "I was almost afraid to make these statements, although there are many living who can corroborate them, until John Muir published the story of his boyhood days, and in it I found the history of such rearing as was my father's, told of as the customary thing among the children of Muir's time; and I have referred many inquirers as to whether this feat were possible, to the Muir book."

All his life, with no thought of fatigue or of inconvenience to himself, Mark Stratton travelled miles uncounted to share what he had learned with those less fortunately situated, by delivering sermons, lectures, talks on civic improvement and politics. To him the love of God could be shown so genuinely in no other way as in the love of his fellowmen. He worshipped beauty: beautiful faces, souls, hearts, beautiful landscapes, trees, animals, flowers. He loved colour: rich, bright colour, and every variation down to the faintest shadings. He was especially fond of red, and the author carefully keeps a cardinal silk handkerchief that he was carrying when stricken with apoplexy at the age of seventy-eight. "It was so like him," she comments, "to have that scrap of vivid colour in his pocket. He never was too busy to fertilize a flower bed or to dig holes for the setting of a tree or bush. A word constantly on his lips was 'tidy.' It applied equally to a woman, a house, a field, or a barn lot. He had a streak of genius in his make-up: the genius of large appreciation. Over inspired Biblical passages, over great books, over sunlit landscapes, over a white violet abloom in deep shade, over a heroic deed of man, I have seen his brow light up, his eyes shine."

Mrs. Porter tells us that her father was constantly reading aloud to his children and to visitors descriptions of the great deeds of men. Two "hair-raisers" she especially remembers with increased heart-beats to this day were the story of John Maynard, who piloted a burning boat to safety while he slowly roasted at the wheel. She says the old thrill comes back when she recalls the inflection of her father's voice as he would cry in imitation of the captain: "John Maynard!" and then give the reply. "Aye, aye, sir!" His other until it sank to a mere gasp: favourite was the story of Clemanthe, and her lover's immortal answer to her question: "Shall we meet again?"

To this mother at forty-six, and this father at fifty, each at intellectual top-notch, every faculty having been stirred for years by the dire stress of Civil War, and the period immediately following, the author was born. From childhood she recalls "thinking things which she felt should be saved," and frequently tugging at her mother's skirts and begging her to "set down" what the child considered stories and poems. Most of these were some big fact in nature that thrilled her, usually expressed in Biblical terms; for the Bible was read twice a day before the family and helpers, and an average of three services were attended on Sunday.

Mrs. Porter says that her first all-alone effort was printed in wabbly letters on the fly-leaf of an old grammar. It was entitled: "Ode to the Moon." "Not," she comments, "that I had an idea what an 'ode' was, other than that I had heard it discussed in the family together with different forms of poetic expression. The spelling must have been by proxy: but I did know the words I used, what they meant, and the idea I was trying to convey.

"No other farm was ever quite so lovely as the one on which I was born after this father and mother had spent twenty-five years beautifying it," says the author. It was called "Hopewell" after the home of some of her father's British ancestors. The natural location was perfect, the land rolling and hilly, with several flowing springs and little streams crossing it in three directions, while plenty of forest still remained. The days of pioneer struggles were past. The roads were smooth and level as floors, the house and barn commodious; the family rode abroad in a double carriage trimmed in patent leather, drawn by a matched team of gray horses, and sometimes the father "speeded a little" for the delight of the children. "We had comfortable clothing," says Mrs. Porter, "and were getting our joy from life without that pinch of anxiety which must have existed in the beginning, although I know that father and mother always held steady, and took a large measure of joy from life in passing."

Her mother's health, which always had been perfect, broke about the time of the author's first remembrance due to typhoid fever contracted after nursing three of her children through it. She lived for several years, but with continual suffering, amounting at times to positive torture.

So it happened, that led by impulse and aided by an

escape from the training given her sisters, instead of "sitting on a cushion and sewing a fine seam" — the threads of the fabric had to be counted and just so many allowed to each stitch! — this youngest child of a numerous household spent her waking hours with the wild. She followed her father and the boys afield, and when tired out slept on their coats in fence corners, often awaking with shy creatures peering into her face. She wandered where she pleased, amusing herself with birds, flowers, insects, and plays she invented. "By the day," writes the author, "I trotted from one object which attracted me to another, singing a little song of made-up phrases about everything I saw while I waded catching fish, chasing butterflies over clover fields, or following a bird with a hair in its beak; much of the time I carried the inevitable baby for a woman-child, frequently improvised from an ear of corn in the silk, wrapped in catalpa leaf blankets."

She had a corner of the garden under a big Bartlett pear tree for her very own, and each spring she began by planting radishes and lettuce when the gardening was done; and before these had time to sprout she set the same beds full of spring flowers, and so followed out the season. She made special pets of the birds, locating nest after nest, and immediately projecting herself into the daily life of the occupants. "No one," she says, "ever taught me more than that the birds were useful, a gift of God for our protection from insect pests on fruit and crops; and a gift of Grace in their beauty and music, things to be rigidly protected. From this cue I evolved the idea myself that I must be extremely careful, for had not my father tied a 'kerchief over my mouth when he lifted me for a peep into the nest of the humming-bird, and did he not walk softly and whisper when he approached the spot? So I stepped lightly, made no noise, and watched until I knew what a mother bird fed her young before I began dropping bugs, worms, crumbs, and fruit into little red mouths that opened at my tap on the nest quite as readily as at the touch of the feet of the mother bird."

In the nature of this child of the out-of-doors there ran a fibre of care for wild things. It was instinct with her to go slowly, to touch lightly, to deal lovingly with every living thing: flower, moth, bird, or animal. She never gathered great handfuls of frail wild flowers, carried them an hour and threw them away. If she picked any, she took only a few, mostly to lay on her mother's pillow — for she had a habit of drawing comfort from a cinnamon pink or a trillium laid where its delicate fragrance reached her with every breath. "I am quite sure," Mrs. Porter writes, "that I never in my life, in picking flowers, dragged up the plant by the roots, as I frequently saw other people do. I was taught from infancy to CUT a bloom I wanted. My regular habit was to lift one plant of each kind, especially if it were a species new to me, and set it in my wild-flower garden."

To the birds and flowers the child added moths and butterflies, because she saw them so frequently, the brilliance of colour in yard and garden attracting more than could be found elsewhere. So she grew with the wild, loving, studying, giving all her time. "I fed butterflies sweetened water and rose leaves inside the screen of a cellar window," Mrs. Porter tells us; "doctored all the sick and wounded birds and animals the men brought me from afield; made pets of the baby squirrels and rabbits they carried in for my amusement; collected wild flowers; and as I grew older, gathered arrow points and goose quills for sale in Fort Wayne. So I had the first money I ever earned."

Her father and mother had strong artistic tendencies, although they would have scoffed at the idea themselves, yet the manner in which they laid off their fields, the home they built, the growing things they preserved, the way they planted, the life they led, all go to prove exactly that thing. Their bush — and vine-covered fences crept around the acres they owned in a strip of gaudy colour; their orchard lay in a valley, a square of apple trees in the centre widely bordered by peach, so that it appeared at bloom time like a great pink-bordered white blanket on the face of earth. Swale they might have drained, and would not, made sheets of blue flag, marigold and buttercups. From the home you could not look in any direction without seeing a picture of beauty.

"Last spring," the author writes in a recent letter, "I went back with my mind fully made up to buy that land at any reasonable price, restore it to the exact condition in which I knew it as a child, and finish my life there. I found that the house had been burned, killing all the big trees set by my mother's hands immediately surrounding it. The hills were shorn and ploughed down, filling and obliterating the creeks and springs. Most of the forest had been cut, and stood in corn. My old catalpa in the fence corner beside the road and the Bartlett pear under which I had my wild-flower garden were all that was left of the dooryard, while a few gnarled apple trees remained of the orchard, which had been reset in another place. The garden had been moved, also the lanes; the one creek remaining out of three crossed the meadow at the foot of the orchard. It flowed a sickly current over a dredged bed between bare, straight banks. The whole place seemed worse than a dilapidated graveyard to me. All my love and ten times the money I had at command never could have put back the face of nature as I knew it on that land."

As a child the author had very few books, only three of her own outside of school books. "The markets did not afford the miracles common with the children of today," she adds. "Books are now so numerous, so cheap, and so bewildering in colour and make-up, that I sometimes think our children are losing their perspective and caring for none of them as I loved my few plain little ones filled with short story and poem, almost no illustration. I had a treasure house in the school books of my elders, especially the McGuffey series of Readers from One to Six. For pictures I was driven to the Bible, dictionary, historical works read by my father, agricultural papers, and medical books about cattle and sheep.

"Near the time of my mother's passing we moved from Hopewell to the city of Wabash in order that she might have constant medical attention, and the younger children better opportunities for schooling. Here we had magazines and more books in which I was interested. The one volume in which my heart was enwrapt was a collection of masterpieces of fiction belonging to my eldest sister. It contained 'Paul and Virginia,' 'Undine,' 'Picciola,' 'The Vicar of Wakefield,' 'Pilgrim's Progress,' and several others I soon learned by heart, and the reading and rereading of those exquisitely expressed and conceived stories may have done much in forming high conceptions of what really constitutes literature and in furthering the lofty ideals instilled by my parents. One of these stories formed the basis of my first publicly recognized literary effort."

Reared by people who constantly pointed out every natural beauty, using it wherever possible to drive home a precept, the child lived out-of-doors with the wild almost entirely. If she reported promptly three times a day when the bell rang at meal time, with enough clothing to constitute a decent covering, nothing more was asked until the Sabbath. To be taken from such freedom, her feet shod, her body restricted by as much clothing as ever had been worn on Sunday, shut up in a schoolroom, and set to droning over books, most of which she detested, was the worst punishment ever inflicted upon her she declares. She hated mathematics in any form and spent all her time on natural science, language, and literature. "Friday afternoon," writes Mrs. Porter, "was always taken up with an exercise called 'rhetoricals,' a misnomer as a rule, but let that pass. Each week pupils of one of the four years furnished entertainment for the assembled high school and faculty. Our subjects were always assigned, and we cordially disliked them. This particular day I was to have a paper on 'Mathematical Law.'

"I put off the work until my paper had been called for several times, and so came to Thursday night with excuses and not a line. I was told to bring my work the next morning without fail. I went home in hot anger. Why in all this beautiful world, would they not allow me to do something I could do, and let any one of four members of my class who revelled in mathematics do my subject? That evening I was distracted. 'I can't do a paper on mathematics, and I won't!' I said stoutly; 'but I'll do such a paper on a subject I can write about as will open their foolish eyes and make them see how wrong they are.'"

Before me on the table lay the book I loved, the most wonderful story in which was 'Picciola' by Saintine. Instantly I began to write. Breathlessly I wrote for hours. I exceeded our limit ten times over. The poor Italian Count, the victim of political offences, shut by Napoleon from the wonderful grounds, mansion, and life that were his, restricted to the bare prison walls of Fenestrella, deprived of books and writing material, his one interest in life became a sprout of green, sprung, no doubt, from a seed dropped by a passing bird, between the stone flagging of the prison yard before his window. With him I had watched over it through all the years since I first had access to the book; with him I had prayed for it. I had broken into a cold sweat of fear when the jailer first menaced it; I had hated the wind that bent it roughly, and implored the sun. I had sung a paean of joy at its budding, and worshipped in awe before its thirty perfect blossoms. The Count had named it 'Picciola' — the little one — to me also it was a personal possession. That night we lived the life of our 'little one' over again, the Count and I, and never were our anxieties and our joys more poignant.

"Next morning," says Mrs. Porter, "I dared my crowd to see how long they could remain on the grounds, and yet reach the assembly room before the last toll of the bell. This scheme worked. Coming in so late the principal opened exercises without remembering my paper. Again, at noon, I was as late as I dared be, and I escaped until near the close of the exercises, through which I sat in cold fear. When my name was reached at last the principal looked at me inquiringly and then announced my inspiring mathematical subject. I arose, walked to the front, and made my best bow. Then I said: 'I waited until yesterday because I knew absolutely nothing about my subject' — the audience laughed — 'and I could find nothing either here or in the library at home, so last night I reviewed Saintine's masterpiece, "Picciola."'

"Then instantly I began to read. I was almost paralyzed at my audacity, and with each word I expected to hear a terse little interruption. Imagine my amazement when I heard at the end of the first page: 'Wait a minute!' Of course I waited, and the principal left the room. A moment later she reappeared accompanied by the superintendent of the city schools. 'Begin again,' she said. 'Take your time.'

"I was too amazed to speak. Then thought came in a rush. My paper was good. It was as good as I had believed it. It was better than I had known. I did go on! We took that assembly room and the corps of teachers into our confidence, the Count and I, and told them all that was in our hearts about a little flower that sprang between the paving stones of a prison yard. The Count and I were free spirits. From the book I had learned that. He got into political trouble through it, and I had got into mathematical trouble, and we told our troubles. One instant the room was in laughter, the next the boys bowed their heads, and the girls who had forgotten their handkerchiefs cried in their aprons. For almost sixteen big foolscap pages I held them, and I was eager to go on and tell them more about it when I reached the last line. Never again was a subject forced upon me."

After this incident of her schooldays, what had been inclination before was aroused to determination and the child neglected her lessons to write. A volume of crude verse fashioned after the metre of Meredith's "Lucile," a romantic book in rhyme, and two novels were the fruits of this youthful ardour. Through the sickness and death of a sister, the author missed the last three months of school, but, she remarks, "unlike my schoolmates, I studied harder after leaving school than ever before and in a manner that did me real good. The most that can be said of what education I have is that it is the very best kind in the world for me; the only possible kind that would not ruin a person of my inclinations. The others of my family had been to college; I always have been too thankful for words that circumstances intervened which saved my brain from being run through a groove in company with dozens of others of widely different tastes and mentality. What small measure of success I have had has come through preserving my individual point of view, method of expression, and following in after life the Spartan regulations of my girlhood home. Whatever I have been able to do, has been done through the line of education my father saw fit to give me, and through his and my mother's methods of rearing me.

"My mother went out too soon to know, and my father never saw one of the books; but he knew I was boiling and bubbling like a yeast jar in July over some literary work, and if I timidly slipped to him with a composition, or a faulty poem, he saw good in it, and made suggestions for its betterment. When I wanted to express something in colour, he went to an artist, sketched a design for an easel, personally superintended the carpenter who built it, and provided tuition. On that same easel I painted the water colours for 'Moths of the Limberlost,' and one of the most poignant regrets of my life is that he was not there to see them, and to know that the easel which he built through his faith in me was finally used in illustrating a book.

"If I thought it was music through which I could express myself, he paid for lessons and detected hidden ability that should be developed. Through the days of struggle he stood fast; firm in his belief in me. He was half the battle. It was he who demanded a physical standard that developed strength to endure the rigours of scientific field and darkroom work, and the building of ten books in ten years, five of which were on nature subjects, having my own illustrations, and five novels, literally teeming with natural history, true to nature. It was he who demanded of me from birth the finishing of any task I attempted and who taught me to cultivate patience to watch and wait, even years, if necessary, to find and secure material I wanted. It was he who daily lived before me the life of exactly such a man as I portrayed in 'The Harvester,' and who constantly used every atom of brain and body power to help and to encourage all men to do the same."

Marriage, a home of her own, and a daughter for a time filled the author's hands, but never her whole heart and brain. The book fever lay dormant a while, and then it became a compelling influence. It dominated the life she lived, the cabin she designed for their home, and the books she read. When her daughter was old enough to go to school, Mrs. Porter's time came. Speaking of this period, she says: "I could not afford a maid, but I was very strong, vital to the marrow, and I knew how to manage life to make it meet my needs, thanks to even the small amount I had seen of my mother. I kept a cabin of fourteen rooms, and kept it immaculate. I made most of my daughter's clothes, I kept a conservatory in which there bloomed from three to six hundred bulbs every winter, tended a house of canaries and linnets, and cooked and washed dishes besides three times a day. In my spare time (mark the word, there was time to spare else the books never would have been written and the pictures made) I mastered photography to such a degree that the manufacturers of one of our finest brands of print paper once sent the manager of their factory to me to learn how I handled it. He frankly said that they could obtain no such results with it as I did. He wanted to see my darkroom, examine my paraphernalia, and have me tell him exactly how I worked. As I was using the family bathroom for a darkroom and washing negatives and prints on turkey platters in the kitchen, I was rather put to it when it came to giving an exhibition. It was scarcely my fault if men could not handle the paper they manufactured so that it produced the results that I obtained, so I said I thought the difference might lie in the chemical properties of the water, and sent this man on his way satisfied. Possibly it did. But I have a shrewd suspicion it lay in high-grade plates, a careful exposure, judicious development, with self-compounded chemicals straight from the factory, and C.P. I think plates swabbed with wet cotton before development, intensified if of short exposure, and thoroughly swabbed again before drying, had much to do with it; and paper handled in the same painstaking manner had more. I have hundreds of negatives in my closet made twelve years ago, in perfect condition for printing from to-day, and I never have lost a plate through fog from imperfect development and hasty washing; so my little mother's rule of 'whatsoever thy hands find to do, do it with thy might,' held good in photography."

Thus had Mrs. Porter made time to study and to write, and editors began to accept what she sent them with little if any changes. She began by sending photographic and natural history hints to Recreation, and with the first installment was asked to take charge of the department and furnish material each month for which she was to be paid at current prices in high-grade photographic material. We can form some idea of the work she did under this arrangement from the fact that she had over one thousand dollars' worth of equipment at the end of the first year. The second year she increased this by five hundred, and then accepted a place on the natural history staff of Outing, working closely with Mr. Casper Whitney. After a year of this helpful experience Mrs. Porter began to turn her attention to what she calls "nature studies sugar coated with fiction." Mixing some childhood fact with a large degree of grown-up fiction, she wrote a little story entitled "Laddie, the Princess, and the Pie."

"I was abnormally sensitive," says the author, "about trying to accomplish any given thing and failing. I had been taught in my home that it was black disgrace to undertake anything and fail. My husband owned a drug and book store that carried magazines, and it was not possible to conduct departments in any of them and not have it known; but only a few people in our locality read these publications, none of them were interested in nature photography, or natural science, so what I was trying to do was not realized even by my own family.

"With them I was much more timid than with the neighbours. Least of all did I want to fail before my man Person and my daughter and our respective families; so I worked in secret, sent in my material, and kept as quiet about it as possible. On Outing I had graduated from the camera department to an illustrated article each month, and as this kept up the year round, and few illustrations could be made in winter, it meant that I must secure enough photographs of wild life in summer to last during the part of the year when few were to be had.

"Every fair day I spent afield, and my little black horse and load of cameras, ropes, and ladders became a familiar sight to the country folk of the Limberlost, in Rainbow Bottom, the Canoper, on the banks of the Wabash, in woods and thickets and beside the roads; but few people understood what I was trying to do, none of them what it would mean were I to succeed. Being so afraid of failure and the inevitable ridicule in a community where I was already severely criticised on account of my ideas of housekeeping, dress, and social customs, I purposely kept everything I did as quiet as possible. It had to be known that I was interested in everything afield, and making pictures; also that I was writing field sketches for nature publications, but little was thought of it, save as one more, peculiarity, in me. So when my little story was finished I went to our store and looked over the magazines. I chose one to which we did not subscribe, having an attractive cover, good type, and paper, and on the back of an old envelope, behind the counter, I scribbled: Perriton Maxwell, 116 Nassau Street, New York, and sent my story on its way.

"Then I took a bold step, the first in my self-emancipation. Money was beginning to come in, and I had some in my purse of my very own that I had earned when no one even knew I was working. I argued that if I kept my family so comfortable that they missed nothing from their usual routine, it was my right to do what I could toward furthering my personal ambitions in what time I could save from my housework. And until I could earn enough to hire capable people to take my place, I held rigidly to that rule. I who waded morass, fought quicksands, crept, worked from ladders high in air, and crossed water on improvised rafts without a tremor, slipped with many misgivings into the postoffice and rented a box for myself, so that if I met with failure my husband and the men in the bank need not know what I had attempted. That was early May; all summer I waited. I had heard that it required a long time for an editor to read and to pass on matter sent him; but my waiting did seem out of all reason. I was too busy keeping my cabin and doing field work to repine; but I decided in my own mind that Mr. Maxwell was a 'mean old thing' to throw away my story and keep the return postage. Besides, I was deeply chagrined, for I had thought quite well of my effort myself, and this seemed to prove that I did not know even the first principles of what would be considered an interesting story.

"Then one day in September I went into our store on an errand and the manager said to me: 'I read your story in the Metropolitan last night. It was great! Did you ever write any fiction before?'

"My head whirled, but I had learned to keep my own counsels, so I said as lightly as I could, while my heart beat until I feared he could hear it: 'No. Just a simple little thing! Have you any spare copies? My sister might want one.'

"He supplied me, so I hurried home, and shutting myself in the library, I sat down to look my first attempt at fiction in the face. I quite agreed with the manager that it was 'great.' Then I wrote Mr. Maxwell a note telling him that I had seen my story in his magazine, and saying that I was glad he liked it enough to use it. I had not known a letter could reach New York and bring a reply so quickly as his answer came. It was a letter that warmed the deep of my heart. Mr. Maxwell wrote that he liked my story very much, but the office boy had lost or destroyed my address with the wrappings, so after waiting a reasonable length of time to hear from me, he had illustrated it the best he could, and printed it. He wrote that so many people had spoken to him of a new, fresh note in it, that he wished me to consider doing him another in a similar vein for a Christmas leader and he enclosed my very first check for fiction.

"So I wrote: 'How Laddie and the Princess Spelled Down at the Christmas Bee.' Mr. Maxwell was pleased to accept that also, with what I considered high praise, and to ask me to furnish the illustrations. He specified that he wanted a frontispiece, head and tail pieces, and six or seven other illustrations. Counting out the time for his letter to reach me, and the material to return, I was left with just ONE day in which to secure the pictures. They had to be of people costumed in the time of the early seventies and I was short of print paper and chemicals. First, I telephoned to Fort Wayne for the material I wanted to be sent without fail on the afternoon train. Then I drove to the homes of the people I wished to use for subjects and made appointments for sittings, and ransacked the cabin for costumes. The letter came on the eight A.M. train. At ten o'clock I was photographing Colonel Lupton beside my dining-room fireplace for the father in the story. At eleven I was dressing and posing Miss Lizzie Huart for the princess. At twelve I was picturing in one of my bed rooms a child who served finely for Little Sister, and an hour later the same child in a cemetery three miles in the country where I used mounted butterflies from my cases, and potted plants carried from my conservatory, for a graveyard scene. The time was early November, but God granted sunshine that day, and short focus blurred the background. At four o'clock I was at the schoolhouse, and in the best-lighted room with five or six models, I was working on the spelling bee scenes. By six I was in the darkroom developing and drying these plates, every one of which was good enough to use. I did my best work with printing-out paper, but I was compelled to use a developing paper in this extremity, because it could be worked with much more speed, dried a little between blotters, and mounted. At three o'clock in the morning I was typing the quotations for the pictures, at four the parcel stood in the hall for the six o'clock train, and I realized that I wanted a drink, food, and sleep, for I had not stopped a second for anything from the time of reading Mr. Maxwell's letter until his order was ready to mail. For the following ten years I was equally prompt in doing all work I undertook, whether pictures or manuscript, without a thought of consideration for self; and I disappointed the confident expectations of my nearest and dearest by remaining sane, normal, and almost without exception the healthiest woman they knew."

This story and its pictures were much praised, and in the following year the author was asked for several stories, and even used bird pictures and natural history sketches, quite an innovation for a magazine at that time. With this encouragement she wrote and illustrated a short story of about ten thousand words, and sent it to the Century. Richard Watson Gilder advised Mrs. Porter to enlarge it to book size, which she did. This book is "The Cardinal." Following Mr. Gilder's advice, she recast the tale and, starting with the mangled body of a cardinal some marksman had left in the road she was travelling, in a fervour of love for the birds and indignation at the hunter, she told the Cardinal's life history in these pages.

The story was promptly accepted and the book was published with very beautiful half-tones, and cardinal buckram cover. Incidentally, neither the author's husband nor daughter had the slightest idea she was attempting to write a book until work had progressed to that stage where she could not make a legal contract without her husband's signature. During the ten years of its life this book has gone through eight different editions, varying in form and make-up from the birds in exquisite colour, as colour work advanced and became feasible, to a binding of beautiful red morocco, a number of editions of differing design intervening. One was tried in gray binding, the colour of the female cardinal, with the red male used as an inset. Another was woodsgreen with the red male, and another red with a wild rose design stamped in. There is a British edition published by Hodder and Stoughton. All of these had the author's own illustrations which authorities agree are the most complete studies of the home life and relations of a pair of birds ever published.

The story of these illustrations in "The Cardinal" and how the author got them will be a revelation to most readers. Mrs. Porter set out to make this the most complete set of bird illustrations ever secured, in an effort to awaken people to the wonder and beauty and value of the birds. She had worked around half a dozen nests for two years and had carried a lemon tree from her conservatory to the location of one nest, buried the tub, and introduced the branches among those the birds used in approaching their home that she might secure proper illustrations for the opening chapter, which was placed in the South. When the complete bird series was finished, the difficult work over, and there remained only a few characteristic Wabash River studies of flowers, vines, and bushes for chapter tail pieces to be secured, the author "met her Jonah," and her escape was little short of a miracle.

After a particularly strenuous spring afield, one teeming day in early August she spent the morning in the river bottom beside the Wabash. A heavy rain followed by August sun soon had her dripping while she made several studies of wild morning glories, but she was particularly careful to wrap up and drive slowly going home, so that she would not chill. In the afternoon the author went to the river northeast of town to secure mallow pictures for another chapter, and after working in burning sun on the river bank until exhausted, she several times waded the river to examine bushes on the opposite bank. On the way home she had a severe chill, and for the following three weeks lay twisted in the convulsions of congestion, insensible most of the time. Skilled doctors and nurses did their best, which they admitted would have availed nothing if the patient had not had a constitution without a flaw upon which to work.

"This is the history," said Mrs. Porter, "of one little tail piece among the pictures. There were about thirty others, none so strenuous, but none easy, each having a living, fighting history for me. If I were to give in detail the story of the two years' work required to secure the set of bird studies illustrating 'The Cardinal,' it would make a much larger book than the life of the bird."

"The Cardinal" was published in June of 1903. On the 20th of October, 1904, "Freckles" appeared. Mrs. Porter had been delving afield with all her heart and strength for several years, and in the course of her work had spent every other day for three months in the Limberlost swamp, making a series of studies of the nest of a black vulture. Early in her married life she had met a Scotch lumberman, who told her of the swamp and of securing fine timber there for Canadian shipbuilders, and later when she had moved to within less than a mile of its northern boundary, she met a man who was buying curly maple, black walnut, golden oak, wild cherry, and other wood extremely valuable for a big furniture factory in Grand Rapids. There was one particular woman, of all those the author worked among, who exercised herself most concerning her. She never failed to come out if she saw her driving down the lane to the woods, and caution her to be careful. If she felt that Mrs. Porter had become interested and forgotten that it was long past meal time, she would send out food and water or buttermilk to refresh her. She had her family posted, and if any of them saw a bird with a straw or a hair in its beak, they followed until they found its location. It was her husband who drove the stake and ploughed around the killdeer nest in the cornfield to save it for the author; and he did many other acts of kindness without understanding exactly what he was doing or why. "Merely that I wanted certain things was enough for those people," writes Mrs. Porter. "Without question they helped me in every way their big hearts could suggest to them, because they loved to be kind, and to be generous was natural with them. The woman was busy keeping house and mothering a big brood, and every living creature that came her way, besides. She took me in, and I put her soul, body, red head, and all, into Sarah Duncan. The lumber and furniture man I combined in McLean. Freckles was a composite of certain ideals and my own field experiences, merged with those of Mr. Bob Burdette Black, who, at the expense of much time and careful work, had done more for me than any other ten men afield. The Angel was an idealized picture of my daughter.

"I dedicated the book to my husband, Mr. Charles Darwin Porter, for several reasons, the chiefest being that he deserved it. When word was brought me by lumbermen of the nest of the Black Vulture in the Limberlost, I hastened to tell my husband the wonderful story of the big black bird, the downy white baby, the pale blue egg, and to beg back a rashly made promise not to work in the Limberlost. Being a natural history enthusiast himself, he agreed that I must go; but he qualified the assent with the proviso that no one less careful of me than he, might accompany me there. His business had forced him to allow me to work alone, with hired guides or the help of oilmen and farmers elsewhere; but a Limberlost trip at that time was not to be joked about. It had not been shorn, branded, and tamed. There were most excellent reasons why I should not go there. Much of it was impenetrable. Only a few trees had been taken out; oilmen were just invading it. In its physical aspect it was a treacherous swamp and quagmire filled with every plant, animal, and human danger known in the worst of such locations in the Central States.

"A rod inside the swamp on a road leading to an oil well we mired to the carriage hubs. I shielded my camera in my arms and before we reached the well I thought the conveyance would be torn to pieces and the horse stalled. At the well we started on foot, Mr. Porter in kneeboots, I in waist-high waders. The time was late June; we forced our way between steaming, fetid pools, through swarms of gnats, flies, mosquitoes, poisonous insects, keeping a sharp watch for rattlesnakes. We sank ankle deep at every step, and logs we thought solid broke under us. Our progress was a steady succession of prying and pulling each other to the surface. Our clothing was wringing wet, and the exposed parts of our bodies lumpy with bites and stings. My husband found the tree, cleared the opening to the great prostrate log, traversed its unspeakable odours for nearly forty feet to its farthest recess, and brought the baby and egg to the light in his leaf-lined hat.

"We could endure the location only by dipping napkins in deodorant and binding them over our mouths and nostrils. Every third day for almost three months we made this trip, until Little Chicken was able to take wing. Of course we soon made a road to the tree, grew accustomed to the disagreeable features of the swamp and contemptuously familiar with its dangers, so that I worked anywhere in it I chose with other assistance; but no trip was so hard and disagreeable as the first. Mr. Porter insisted upon finishing the Little Chicken series, so that 'deserve' is a poor word for any honour that might accrue to him for his part in the book."

This was the nucleus of the book, but the story itself originated from the fact that one day, while leaving the swamp, a big feather with a shaft over twenty inches long came spinning and swirling earthward and fell in the author's path. Instantly she looked upward to locate the bird, which from the size and formation of the quill could have been nothing but an eagle; her eyes, well trained and fairly keen though they were, could not see the bird, which must have been soaring above range. Familiar with the life of the vulture family, the author changed the bird from which the feather fell to that described in "Freckles." Mrs. Porter had the old swamp at that time practically untouched, and all its traditions to work upon and stores of natural history material. This falling feather began the book which in a few days she had definitely planned and in six months completely written. Her title for it was "The Falling Feather," that tangible thing which came drifting down from Nowhere, just as the boy came, and she has always regretted the change to "Freckles." John Murray publishes a British edition of this book which is even better liked in Ireland and Scotland than in England.

As "The Cardinal" was published originally not by Doubleday, Page & Company, but by another firm, the author had talked over with the latter house the scheme of "Freckles" and it had been agreed to publish the story as soon as Mrs. Porter was ready. How the book finally came to Doubleday, Page & Company she recounts as follows:

"By the time 'Freckles' was finished, I had exercised my woman's prerogative and 'changed my mind'; so I sent the manuscript to Doubleday, Page & Company, who accepted it. They liked it well enough to take a special interest in it and to bring it out with greater expense than it was at all customary to put upon a novel at that time; and this in face of the fact that they had repeatedly warned me that the nature work in it would kill fully half its chances with the public. Mr. F.N. Doubleday, starting on a trip to the Bahamas, remarked that he would like to take a manuscript with him to read, and the office force decided to put 'Freckles' into his grip. The story of the plucky young chap won his way to the heart of the publishers, under a silk cotton tree, 'neath bright southern skies, and made such a friend of him that through the years of its book-life it has been the object of special attention. Mr. George Doran gave me a photograph which Mr. Horace MacFarland made of Mr. Doubleday during this reading of the Mss. of 'Freckles' which is especially interesting."

That more than 2,000,000 readers have found pleasure and profit in Mrs. Porter's books is a cause for particular gratification. These stories all have, as a fundamental reason of their existence, the author's great love of nature. To have imparted this love to others — to have inspired many hundreds of thousands to look for the first time with seeing eyes at the pageant of the out-of-doors — is a satisfaction that must endure. For the part of the publishers, they began their business by issuing "Nature Books" at a time when the sale of such works was problematical. As their tastes and inclinations were along the same lines which Mrs. Porter loved to follow, it gave them great pleasure to be associated with her books which opened the eyes of so great a public to new and worthy fields of enjoyment.

The history of "Freckles" is unique. The publishers had inserted marginal drawings on many pages, but these, instead of attracting attention to the nature charm of the book, seemed to have exactly a contrary effect. The public wanted a novel. The illustrations made it appear to be a nature book, and it required three long slow years for "Freckles" to pass from hand to hand and prove that there really was a novel between the covers, but that it was a story that took its own time and wound slowly toward its end, stopping its leisurely course for bird, flower, lichen face, blue sky, perfumed wind, and the closest intimacies of the daily life of common folk. Ten years have wrought a great change in the sentiment against nature work and the interest in it. Thousands who then looked upon the world with unobserving eyes are now straining every nerve to accumulate enough to be able to end life where they may have bird, flower, and tree for daily companions.

Mrs. Porter's account of the advice she received at this time is particularly interesting. Three editors who read "Freckles" before it was published offered to produce it, but all of them expressed precisely the same opinion: "The book will never sell well as it is. If you want to live from the proceeds of your work, if you want to sell even moderately, you must CUT OUT THE NATURE STUFF." "Now to PUT IN THE NATURE STUFF," continues the author, "was the express purpose for which the book had been written. I had had one year's experience with 'The Song of the Cardinal,' frankly a nature book, and from the start I realized that I never could reach the audience I wanted with a book on nature alone. To spend time writing a book based wholly upon human passion and its outworking I would not. So I compromised on a book into which I put all the nature work that came naturally within its scope, and seasoned it with little bits of imagination and straight copy from the lives of men and women I had known intimately, folk who lived in a simple, common way with which I was familiar. So I said to my publishers: 'I will write the books exactly as they take shape in my mind. You publish them. I know they will sell enough that you will not lose. If I do not make over six hundred dollars on a book I shall never utter a complaint. Make up my work as I think it should be and leave it to the people as to what kind of book they will take into their hearts and homes.' I altered 'Freckles' slightly, but from that time on we worked on this agreement.

"My years of nature work have not been without considerable insight into human nature, as well," continues Mrs. Porter. "I know its failings, its inborn tendencies, its weaknesses, its failures, its depth of crime; and the people who feel called upon to spend their time analyzing, digging into, and uncovering these sources of depravity have that privilege, more's the pity! If I had my way about it, this is a privilege no one could have in books intended for indiscriminate circulation. I stand squarely for book censorship, and I firmly believe that with a few more years of such books, as half a dozen I could mention, public opinion will demand this very thing. My life has been fortunate in one glad way: I have lived mostly in the country and worked in the woods. For every bad man and woman I have ever known, I have met, lived with, and am intimately acquainted with an overwhelming number of thoroughly clean and decent people who still believe in God and cherish high ideals, and it is UPON THE LIVES OF THESE THAT I BASE WHAT I WRITE. To contend that this does not produce a picture true to life is idiocy. It does. It produces a picture true to ideal life; to the best that good men and good women can do at level best.

"I care very little for the magazine or newspaper critics who proclaim that there is no such thing as a moral man, and that my pictures of life are sentimental and idealized. They are! And I glory in them! They are straight, living pictures from the lives of men and women of morals, honour, and loving kindness. They form 'idealized pictures of life' because they are copies from life where it touches religion, chastity, love, home, and hope of heaven ultimately. None of these roads leads to publicity and the divorce court. They all end in the shelter and seclusion of a home.

"Such a big majority of book critics and authors have begun to teach, whether they really believe it or not, that no book is TRUE TO LIFE unless it is true to the WORST IN LIFE, that the idea has infected even the women."

In 1906, having seen a few of Mrs. Porter's studies of bird life, Mr. Edward Bok telegraphed the author asking to meet him in Chicago. She had a big portfolio of fine prints from plates for which she had gone to the last extremity of painstaking care, and the result was an order from Mr. Bok for a six months' series in the Ladies' Home Journal of the author's best bird studies accompanied by descriptions of how she secured them. This material was later put in book form under the title, "What I Have Done with Birds," and is regarded as authoritative on the subject of bird photography and bird life, for in truth it covers every phase of the life of the birds described, and contains much of other nature subjects.

By this time Mrs. Porter had made a contract with her publishers to alternate her books. She agreed to do a nature book for love, and then, by way of compromise, a piece of nature work spiced with enough fiction to tempt her class of readers. In this way she hoped that they would absorb enough of the nature work while reading the fiction to send them afield, and at the same time keep in their minds her picture of what she considers the only life worth living. She was still assured that only a straight novel would "pay," but she was living, meeting all her expenses, giving her family many luxuries, and saving a little sum for a rainy day she foresaw on her horoscope. To be comfortably clothed and fed, to have time and tools for her work, is all she ever has asked of life.

Among Mrs. Porter's readers "At the Foot of the Rainbow" stands as perhaps the author's strongest piece of fiction.

In August of 1909 two books on which the author had been working for years culminated at the same time: a nature novel, and a straight nature book. The novel was, in a way, a continuation of "Freckles," filled as usual with wood lore, but more concerned with moths than birds. Mrs. Porter had been finding and picturing exquisite big night flyers during several years of field work among the birds, and from what she could have readily done with them she saw how it would be possible for a girl rightly constituted and environed to make a living, and a good one, at such work. So was conceived "A Girl of the Limberlost." "This comes fairly close to my idea of a good book," she writes. "No possible harm can be done any one in reading it. The book can, and does, present a hundred pictures that will draw any reader in closer touch with nature and the Almighty, my primal object in each line I write. The human side of the book is as close a character study as I am capable of making. I regard the character of Mrs. Comstock as the best thought-out and the cleanest-cut study of human nature I have so far been able to do. Perhaps the best justification of my idea of this book came to me recently when I received an application from the President for permission to translate it into Arabic, as the first book to be used in an effort to introduce our methods of nature study into the College of Cairo."

Hodder and Stoughton of London published the British edition of this work.

At the same time that "A Girl of the Limberlost" was published there appeared the book called "Birds of the Bible." This volume took shape slowly. The author made a long search for each bird mentioned in the Bible, how often, where, why; each quotation concerning it in the whole book, every abstract reference, why made, by whom, and what it meant. Then slowly dawned the sane and true things said of birds in the Bible compared with the amazing statements of Aristotle, Aristophanes, Pliny, and other writers of about the same period in pagan nations. This led to a search for the dawn of bird history and for the very first pictures preserved of them. On this book the author expended more work than on any other she has ever written.

In 1911 two more books for which Mrs. Porter had gathered material for long periods came to a conclusion on the same date: "Music of the Wild" and "The Harvester." The latter of these was a nature novel; the other a frank nature book, filled with all outdoors — a special study of the sounds one hears in fields and forests, and photographic reproductions of the musicians and their instruments.

The idea of "The Harvester" was suggested to the author by an editor who wanted a magazine article, with human interest in it, about the ginseng diggers in her part of the country. Mr. Porter had bought ginseng for years for a drug store he owned; there were several people he knew still gathering it for market, and growing it was becoming a good business all over the country. Mrs. Porter learned from the United States Pharmacopaeia and from various other sources that the drug was used mostly by the Chinese, and with a wholly mistaken idea of its properties. The strongest thing any medical work will say for ginseng is that it is "A VERY MILD AND SOOTHING DRUG." It seems that the Chinese buy and use it in enormous quantities, in the belief that it is a remedy for almost every disease to which humanity is heir; that it will prolong life, and that it is a wonderful stimulant. Ancient medical works make this statement, laying special emphasis upon its stimulating qualities. The drug does none of these things. Instead of being a stimulant, it comes closer to a sedative. This investigation set the author on the search for other herbs that now are or might be grown as an occupation. Then came the idea of a man who should grow these drugs professionally, and of the sick girl healed by them. "I could have gone to work and started a drug farm myself," remarks Mrs. Porter, "with exactly the same profit and success as the Harvester. I wrote primarily to state that to my personal knowledge, clean, loving men still exist in this world, and that no man is forced to endure the grind of city life if he wills otherwise. Any one who likes, with even such simple means as herbs he can dig from fence corners, may start a drug farm that in a short time will yield him delightful work and independence. I WROTE THE BOOK AS I THOUGHT IT SHOULD BE WRITTEN, TO PROVE MY POINTS AND ESTABLISH MY CONTENTIONS. I THINK IT DID. MEN THE GLOBE AROUND PROMPTLY WROTE ME THAT THEY ALWAYS HAD OBSERVED THE MORAL CODE; OTHERS THAT THE SUBJECT NEVER IN ALL THEIR LIVES HAD BEEN PRESENTED TO THEM FROM MY POINT OF VIEW, BUT NOW THAT IT HAD BEEN, THEY WOULD CHANGE AND DO WHAT THEY COULD TO INFLUENCE ALL MEN TO DO THE SAME."

Messrs. Hodder and Stoughton publish a British edition of "The Harvester," there is an edition in Scandinavian, it was running serially in a German magazine, but for a time at least the German and French editions that were arranged will be stopped by this war, as there was a French edition of "The Song of the Cardinal."

After a short rest, the author began putting into shape a

book for which she had been compiling material since the beginning of field work. From the first study she made of an exquisite big night moth, Mrs. Porter used every opportunity to secure more and representative studies of each family in her territory, and eventually found the work so fascinating that she began hunting cocoons and raising caterpillars in order to secure life histories and make illustrations with fidelity to life. "It seems," comments the author, "that scientists and lepidopterists from the beginning have had no hesitation in describing and using mounted moth and butterfly specimens for book text and illustration, despite the fact that their colours fade rapidly, that the wings are always in unnatural positions, and the bodies shrivelled. I would quite as soon accept the mummy of any particular member of the Rameses family as a fair representation of the living man, as a mounted moth for a live one."

When she failed to secure the moth she wanted in a living and perfect specimen for her studies, the author set out to raise one, making photographic studies from the eggs through the entire life process. There was one June during which she scarcely slept for more than a few hours of daytime the entire month. She turned her bedroom into a hatchery, where were stored the most precious cocoons; and if she lay down at night it was with those she thought would produce moths before morning on her pillow, where she could not fail to hear them emerging. At the first sound she would be up with notebook in hand, and by dawn, busy with cameras. Then she would be forced to hurry to the darkroom and develop her plates in order to be sure that she had a perfect likeness, before releasing the specimen, for she did release all she produced except one pair of each kind, never having sold a moth, personally. Often where the markings were wonderful and complicated, as soon as the wings were fully developed Mrs. Porter copied the living specimen in water colours for her illustrations, frequently making several copies in order to be sure that she laid on the colour enough BRIGHTER than her subject so that when it died it would be exactly the same shade.

"Never in all my life," writes the author, "have I had such

exquisite joy in work as I had in painting the illustrations for this volume of 'Moths of the Limberlost.' Colour work had advanced to such a stage that I knew from the beautiful reproductions in Arthur Rackham's 'Rheingold and Valkyrie' and several other books on the market, that time so spent would not be lost. Mr. Doubleday had assured me personally that I might count on exact reproduction, and such details of type and paper as I chose to select. I used the easel made for me when a girl, under the supervision of my father, and I threw my whole heart into the work of copying each line and delicate shading on those wonderful wings, 'all diamonded with panes of quaint device, innumerable stains and splendid dyes,' as one poet describes them. There were times, when in working a mist of colour over another background, I cut a brush down to three hairs. Some of these illustrations I sent back six and seven times, to be worked over before the illustration plates were exact duplicates of the originals, and my heart ached for the engravers, who must have had Job-like patience; but it did not ache enough to stop me until I felt the reproduction exact. This book tells its own story of long and patient waiting for a specimen, of watching, of disappointments, and triumphs. I love it especially among my book children because it represents my highest ideals in the making of a nature book, and I can take any skeptic afield and prove the truth of the natural history it contains."

In August of 1913 the author's novel "Laddie" was published in New York, London, Sydney and Toronto simultaneously. This book contains the same mixture of romance and nature interest as the others, and is modelled on the same plan of introducing nature objects peculiar to the location, and characters, many of whom are from life, typical of the locality at a given period. The first thing many critics said of it was that "no such people ever existed, and no such life was ever lived." In reply to this the author said: "Of a truth, the home I described in this book I knew to the last grain of wood in the doors, and I painted, it with absolute accuracy; and many of the people I described I knew more intimately than I ever have known any others. TAKEN AS A WHOLE IT REPRESENTS A PERFECTLY FAITHFUL PICTURE OF HOME LIFE,

IN A FAMILY WHO WERE REARED AND EDUCATED EX-ACTLY AS THIS BOOK INDICATES. There was such a man as Laddie, and he was as much bigger and better than my description of him as a real thing is always better than its presentment. The only difference, barring the nature work, between my books and those of many other writers, is that I prefer to describe and to perpetuate the BEST I have known in life; whereas many authors seem to feel that they have no hope of achieving a high literary standing unless they delve in and reproduce the WORST.

"To deny that wrong and pitiful things exist in life is folly, but to believe that these things are made better by promiscuous discussion at the hands of writers who FAIL TO PROVE BY THEIR BOOKS that their viewpoint is either right, clean, or helpful, is close to insanity. If there is to be any error on either side in a book, then God knows it is far better that it should be upon the side of pure sentiment and high ideals than upon that of a too loose discussion of subjects which often open to a large part of the world their first knowledge of such forms of sin, profligate expenditure, and waste of life's best opportunities. There is one great beauty in idealized romance: reading it can make no one worse than he is, while it may help thousands to a cleaner life and higher inspiration than they ever before have known."

Mrs. Porter has written ten books, and it is not out of place here to express her attitude toward them. Each was written, she says, from her heart's best impulses. They are as clean and helpful as she knew how to make them, as beautiful and interesting. She has never spared herself in the least degree, mind or body, when it came to giving her best, and she has never considered money in relation to what she was writing.

During the hard work and exposure of those early years, during rainy days and many nights in the darkroom, she went straight ahead with field work, sending around the globe for books and delving to secure material for such books as "Birds of the Bible," "Music of the Wild," and "Moths of the Limberlost." Every day devoted to such work was "commercially" lost, as publishers did not fail to tell her. But that was the work she could do, and do with exceeding joy. She could do it better pictorially, on account of her lifelong knowledge of living things afield, than any other woman had as yet had the strength and nerve to do it. It was work in which she gloried, and she persisted. "Had I been working for money," comments the author, "not one of these nature books ever would have been written, or an illustration made."

When the public had discovered her and given generous approval to "A Girl of the Limberlost," when "The Harvester" had established a new record, that would have been the time for the author to prove her commercialism by dropping nature work, and plunging headlong into books it would pay to write, and for which many publishers were offering alluring sums. Mrs. Porter's answer was the issuing of such books as "Music of the Wild" and "Moths of the Limberlost." No argument is necessary. Mr. Edward Shuman, formerly critic of the Chicago Record-Herald, was impressed by this method of work and pointed it out in a review. It appealed to Mr. Shuman, when "Moths of the Limberlost" came in for review, following the tremendous success of "The Harvester," that had the author been working for money, she could have written half a dozen more "Harvesters" while putting seven years of field work, on a scientific subject, into a personally illustrated work.

In an interesting passage dealing with her books, Mrs. Porter writes: "I have done three times the work on my books of fiction that I see other writers putting into a novel, in order to make all natural history allusions accurate and to write them in such fashion that they will meet with the commendation of high schools, colleges, and universities using what I write as text books, and for the homes that place them in their libraries. I am perfectly willing to let time and the hearts of the people set my work in its ultimate place. I have no delusions concerning it.

"To my way of thinking and working the greatest service a piece of fiction can do any reader is to leave him with a higher ideal of life than he had when he began. If in one small degree it shows him where he can be a gentler, saner, cleaner, kindlier man, it is a wonder-working book. If it opens his eyes to one beauty in nature he never saw for himself, and leads him one step toward the God of the Universe, it is a beneficial book, for one step into the miracles of nature leads to that long walk, the glories of which so strengthen even a boy who thinks he is dying, that he faces his struggle like a gladiator."

During the past ten years thousands of people have sent the author word that through her books they have been led afield and to their first realization of the beauties of nature her mail brings an average of ten such letters a day, mostly from students, teachers, and professional people of our largest cities. It can probably be said in all truth of her nature books and nature novels, that in the past ten years they have sent more people afield than all the scientific writings of the same period. That is a big statement, but it is very likely pretty close to the truth. Mrs. Porter has been asked by two London and one Edinburgh publishers for the privilege of bringing out complete sets of her nature books, but as yet she has not felt ready to do this.

In bringing this sketch of Gene Stratton-Porter to a close it will be interesting to quote the author's own words describing the Limberlost Swamp, its gradual disappearance under the encroachments of business, and her removal to a new field even richer in natural beauties. She says: "In the beginning of the end a great swamp region lay in north-eastern Indiana. Its head was in what is now Noble and DeKalb counties; its body in Allen and Wells, and its feet in southern Adams and northern Jay The Limberlost lies at the foot and was, when I settled near it, EXACTLY AS DE-SCRIBED IN MY BOOKS. The process of dismantling it was told in, Freckles, to start with, carried on in 'A Girl of the Limberlost,' and finished in 'Moths of the Limberlost.' Now it has so completely fallen prey to commercialism through the devastation of lumbermen, oilmen, and farmers, that I have been forced to move my working territory and build a new cabin about seventy miles north, at the head of the swamp in Noble county, where there are many lakes, miles of unbroken marsh, and a far greater wealth of plant and animal life than existed during my time in the southern part. At the north end every bird that frequents the Central States is to be found.

Here grow in profusion many orchids, fringed gentians, cardinal flowers, turtle heads, starry campions, purple gerardias, and grass of Parnassus. In one season I have located here almost every flower named in the botanies as native to these regions and several that I can find in no book in my library.

"But this change of territory involves the purchase of fifteen acres of forest and orchard land, on a lake shore in marsh country. It means the building of a permanent, all-year-round home, which will provide the comforts of life for my family and furnish a workshop consisting of a library, a photographic darkroom and negative closet, and a printing room for me. I could live in such a home as I could provide on the income from my nature work alone; but when my working grounds were cleared, drained and ploughed up, literally wiped from the face of the earth, I never could have moved to new country had it not been for the earnings of the novels, which I now spend, and always have spent, in great part UPON MY NATURE WORK. Based on this plan of work and life I have written ten books, and 'please God I live so long,' I shall write ten more. Possibly every one of them will be located in northern Indiana. Each one will be filled with all the field and woods legitimately falling to its location and peopled with the best men and women I have known."

Made in the USA
Coppell, TX
23 April 2021

54116247R00023